# Oftentimes a Reason

## Poems and Reflections

Judy Stavnshoj

PublishAmerica
Baltimore

First printing

Photography and illustrations by Max Stavnshoj

PublishAmerica has allowed this work to remain exactly as the author intended, verbatim, without editorial input.

ISBN: 978-1-60749-673-1
PUBLISHED BY PUBLISHAMERICA, LLLP
www.publishamerica.com
Baltimore

Printed in the United States of America

Thank you to my husband, Max, for his support, help and encouragement to continue on. Then to my sister, Sandy, for her technical assistance. And finally to my son, Rob, for inspiring me to pick up my pencil and begin writing again.

# Oftentimes a Reason

Judy Stavnshoj

# OFTENTIMES A REASON

Yes, life seems cruel at times, but maybe for a reason.
Just as nature is.


The harshness of winter with it unforgiving cold and darkness.
Stripping the foliage of its leaves to stand naked against the wind.
To lay dormant only to find itself being covered gently
with the pureness of snow.
A blanket of warmth to protect it. Time to rest.


The warmth of spring that melts the blanket of snow
allowing the first sign of life to awaken and spring forth.


Summer, with sunshine and warmth to nourish this life
bringing all into its peak of the cycle.
Plenty of food to nourish the young offspring
giving strength before the seasons change.


Then fall, with darkness approaching,
to slowly shed the life from nature's growth.
To continue the cycle and prepare for the harshness of winter again.


To sleep beneath the warm blanket of snow

# THE WILD FLOWER

How does your garden grow?
To tired of tending at times?
Maybe neglectful in watering and nourishing.
Most often, of a forgiving kind.

When a blossom is crushed, a new one usually springs forth
of more beauty and strength if being of a hearty stock.
Or if not, only to die without a strong support for it.

Is this as we are?
Gaining strength through our troubled times
only to spring forth as a stronger being
or to whither away from burdens to heavy upon us.

From the overgrown garden,
being strangled slowly not able to withstand the heavy burdens
or, to be as the wild flower and flourish?

# SPECIAL MOMENTS AS A CHILD

To journey back in time at a time when there wasn't any,
all we thought of was forever.
Can we recapture the special moments of such a simple time?

To look out over glistening diamonds as the sun shines down upon
the sea, reflecting its power upon us,
hypnotized by the beauty of this.

There is nothing as tranquil as the peaceful sound of the waves and
the graceful slow movement of the sea.

Just as when you pick up a sea shell and put to your ear.
Happiness in your heart as you hear the roar of the sea.

# THE MALLARDS

Once a year, for a short time, they would land in the pond.
He so powerful and mighty, she timid and shy.

Floating in their own private lake, feasting on bread crumbs.
Then bathing and fluffing on the edge of the pond.
What a joy for us to watch.
Looking forward to seeing them each year.

The male, being so protective of her, leading the way.
She, always to follow with total trust.

For several years this ritual took place.
Then one year, she was to land alone
frantic and anxious.
Left alone to fend for herself.
A new life to survive on her own.

Just as when we lose a loved one…
No different than the mallards.

# WINTER'S BLANKET

Is there anything more serene and quiet than
the muffled sound after a snowfall?
Nature, tucked in beneath a winter blanket.

The old growth, not able to withstand the weight,
only to break off and die while the young limbs survive.
Nature, cleansing itself of the old to make room for the young.

Or to look at the family of hares.
Burrowing into the safe haven in the ground.
Sustaining warmth from each other.
The instinct of togetherness for survival.
Something, we may have lost.

Do we want to be as the old and fragile limb,
unable to stand alone without support
or of the family giving each other comfort and strength?
Unyielding to the heavy burdens that may fall upon us.

Beneath the quiet, serene winter blanket, so much life…

# A FRIEND

As I reflect upon the past,
the water was rough and treacherous that knew no direction.
I had not a friend but knew of a person.

The pounding waves that beat against ones soul
are painful yet over a period of time,
seem to soften the stone in which we surround ourselves.

If not allowed to feel,
the stone is sharpened as a shield to protect oneself
only to become yet harder.
Then it is always as only one because it cannot feel anymore.

As I now look at the water it is still rough and treacherous
but flows at an even stride. The stone is not as sharp.

I look for this person but he is gone.
For now, he has become my friend.

# SIMPLICITY

Where do we find the cheery and lighter side of life?
Is it in laughter or money
or maybe even the first spring flower?

To watch it rising up through the ground.
To grasp its first rays of sunshine, it's life.
We nurture it, food and water and watch it grow.
Enjoying each new petal, knowing it will not last forever.

Maybe, if we treated each other this way,
The world would be a better place.

# SEASONS

To sit and listen to the rainfall softly at first
then turning into a heavy pounding upon the rooftop.

The howling of the wind soon to follow,
harshly brushing the weakened limbs of trees to help shed its leaves.
Such a soothing sound to listen to, yet not a welcome sign to see.

Fall and winter are approaching.
The season changing to cleanse the air and
water the thirsty ground in need, after a long summer.
Revitalizing…nature preparing for the forthcoming season.

The flowers, to shed their petals and hide in the ground.
Finding warmth and nourishment
to sustain them until the coldness has passed.

Knowing that nature is preparing
we listen to this peaceful and soothing sound.

# NATURE

The vultures flying low on the lookout for food.
Their good fortune in finding dead carcass to feast upon.
A celebration of death to one and allowing
continuation of life for the other.
Basic Necessity

# HUMAN GREED

On the lookout for more power and wealth,
to pray on the weak causing poverty and hardship.
To feed their addiction never having enough.

Overdoing and stripping nature and society
as it was intended to support all.
Oceans, forests and the air we breathe.

No wonder nature is fighting back to scorn us of wrongdoings.
Her mighty force to humble those who have done wrong.
A force that cannot be won.

Over civilization and self destruction.

# PEACEFUL DREAMS

What do you see when you look out the window?


Summer, coming to an end.
The leaves are starting to fall and the flowers are drooping.
Running out of energy from a busy season.
The squirrels collecting nuts for the long winter soon to come.


How sad to see.
Nature being stripped of its beauty, which we have enjoyed so much.
Summer, the most productive time in life.


But, nature, like us, must rest at times. To lay down our limbs.
Rest, thus giving us strength when needed.
So, maybe we shouldn't be so sad to see the
shedding of life outside our window.


A long rest needed, so that we may enjoy another season.
A season that gives all energy in life…


Yes, to rest with peaceful dreams.

# THE WILLOW

A weeping willow stands naked in winter
with bare limbs falling gracefully.
Waiting until spring to show off its beauty
when young buds will adorn its limbs.
Looking so beautiful and to the touch, the feel of silk.
A time when it is most appealing.

Spring showers arrive to wash away this show
leaving only fallen buds.
Naked again for a short time
until it fans out with green leaves to cover itself.
Just as youth and its beauty

Eventually the tree grows old,
not able to produce this show which is so appealing to the eye
To stand naked with brittle limbs and few green leaves.

Left to weep for what is and the past that is no more.

# A CRY

The noise of the mighty thunderstorm lashing out for all to hear
Such a show of anger.

The sky opens up to cry out
As we seek shelter from the unknown and overpowering noise.
Such a mighty roar, with heavy tears to follow
Smashing into the earth
Crushing all beneath it of lesser strength.
To lie down against the pounding of the tears

Why is this?
Nature may be feeding the thirsty after a long season of sun.
A show of power that nature is still in command.
To feed the drought stricken limbs that will rise up and thrive again.

Listen and take notice of this mighty roar, it is for all to hear and feel.
Maybe this anger is a cry for help before all is destroyed.

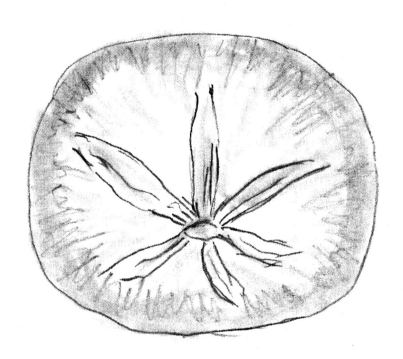

# AS A CHILD AGAIN

To walk the beach and feel the hot sand under foot.
The warm salt breeze to tickle your skin.

To look for seashells, build a castle or gaze out over the sea.

So much time. Just as a young child.
To forget yesterday and live for and enjoy the adventures of the day.

You've raised your family, devoting the best of a lifetime.
They will survive with or without your worry
as they know you will always be there for them with loving thoughts
as consistent as the forever rhythm of the sea.

For this,
your children will always hear the same sound of the sea as you do,
even if they are not beside you.

So, enjoy life once again, as a child.
For now, you have the wisdom to know that which you cannot change
and the courage to live by this.

# CHERISHED MEMORIES

Looking out upon the sea, reflecting on pleasant memories of the past.
So far away now, only a memory to be cherished.


Summers at the beach as children not realizing what a treasure we had,
until it was gone.
To gently pick up the little sand crabs so as not to harm their fragile legs.
Or, to build a castle in the sand only to have it washed away
but knowing we could build another the next day.
To watch a herd of deer so quiet and peaceful,
Gathering at the shoreline for sea salt.


All taken for granted.

# 20 YEARS LATER

Today the pollution and toxins greet us at the shoreline.
We have taken from nature and ourselves.
The life cycle has become unbalanced.
What you love and cherish today
must be kept sacred to survive tomorrow.

Is it better to have cherished memories
knowing they will never return as before
or, to not have known what there is to cherish?

# TO GATHER COMFORT

God is thought of in many forms, to hear, see and feel.

To hear the gentle waves upon the shore to sooth the human soul.
To watch a soaring eagle showing his majestic self,
such a powerful sight.
To listen to the birds singing their beautiful songs in harmony
with the chattering squirrels.
Living creatures we share our world with.

Maybe the sun for warmth and energy giving life to all.
Water to satisfy ones thirst or to listen to the babbling brook.
To feel the gentle stroke of the wind upon ones skin.

So yes, we all have a God in many forms
to whom we gather comfort from.

# AT PEACE

The years seem to pass by so quickly.
What have we accomplished?
A dream not fulfilled and yet still to strive for or,
contentment with life for what we have accomplished.

Maybe, we ask of ourselves too much,
never able to fill our dreams.

Wouldn't it be better
to feel contentment with what we have accomplished
not dwell upon what we have not?

# TO DREAM

At the beach, a young child sits in the sand building a sandcastle.
Having the innocence of a young child, full of imagination,
he goes about building a dream of his own.
Careful planning and patience, so his castle is just how he wants it.

Then the tide comes in to slowly wash away his dreams.
Not understanding, he sheds many tears.
He will return tomorrow to build another.
The waves will not stop him. He will build a bigger and stronger one.

How many waves must wash away our dreams before one tires of trying?
For some, not many.
Others learn to compromise and build around what we cannot control
or may not have the strength to change.

The child grows up and as a young man remembers the sandcastle.
He has had to compromise and build his life on safer ground.

Though, in his dreams, he still wishes to build his castle in the sand.

# MOTHER

A friend is indeed, often of need.
Who is this person who will listen with an open mind
and put you at ease during times of doubt or trouble?

To share a laugh or share a tear does not matter
as long as it is shared
You open yourselves up to one another with total trust.
You are not judged upon what you say
but listened to with understanding.

There is a bond between them
that enables each to share their thoughts without words spoken.
For this, they share in life, pain and happiness.
One feeling as the other.

This is a gift not all of us have and can easily be taken for granted.
Unfortunately, it is often only during times of need
we realize just how precious this gift is.

Your friend has always been there, and this will always be.
You will try to pass this gift along.

"This most precious gift from your mother"

# FATHER

He worked hard his whole life tending to his garden.
Having the patience and taking the time to care and feed
and pull the weeds that can strangle their fragile roots.

When a storm would pass, crushing the blossoms,
he was always there to pick up the shedding tears of the petals.
To help them rise up again and regain strength from the sun.

Now, he can look back and see the rewards of his hard work.
The seeds of love that he planted and cared for,
get carried down through generations.
They do not get lost in the wind but replant themselves,
only to start the cycle over.

Because of his love,
the mature flowers follow his path and give of themselves
to help the new seedlings grow strong roots to flourish into strong flowers.

This giving is the meaning of a fathers love.

# MIDDLE AGE

You stop telling your children what to do
because you finally realize they don't and never have listened.

You reminisce about your younger days as if they were yesterday,
but, are outdated today.

A hangover is something you avoid.
It really just isn't fun.

You give up wishing you had done something you hadn't.
Now you don't care.

You're concerned about health insurance because you use it.

You're not concerned about dental insurance
because you now wear dentures.

Vacation involves more expensive accommodations.
You now use your room,
before it was just for showering and sleeping.

You wish you knew what you know now
and you'd do everything differently.

However, on a brighter note…


You're climbing the ladder and
soon you will reach the ripe golden age of retirement.
Able to retire and live with some comfort and security.
Yes, you'll be able to receive what you have been working for
your entire life


SOCIAL SECURITY.


Or, is it like magic, the rabbit in the hat. Where did it go?

# THE COTTON TOPS

There is a species of animal that all migrate South in the winter time. Most of them go to
Florida. They are known as the cotton top. The shopping malls, beaches and restaurants
are full of them. What makes them so rare is that their habits are a little different than the
more common species known as human.

This rare breed when all congregated together in a similar place, seem to not have any
cares anymore. They can endlessly stroll for long periods of time and seem to enjoy what
they are not doing. Whereas the human has a time frame to live by. Places to go and
things to get accomplished. The Cotton Top also has a very peculiar method of driving.
Darting in and out of traffic without looking, speeding down the street in a 25 mph zone
or going 25 in a 60 mph zone. All things which the common human cannot begin to
understand, nor do we want to.

Anyway, they have chosen a warm place where not as many pieces of clothing are
required, thus enabling them to grow more brown freckles. This seems to be a status quo
among them… The more brown freckles the more strolling that has been done.

Oh well, after a while they get tired of the warm weather and of doing nothing so they
eventually go home to their families where they learn to become like a human again. We
help them by adding a little stress to their lives along with giving them some
responsibilities.

Then the cycle starts over again. They have the need to stroll endlessly along with all the
other Cotton tops. We miss them when they are gone and look forward to when they
return in the spring.

# A NEW SEASON

The long waited season, finally to arrive,
with all the liveliness from the fresh new young.

Be it the young chicks learning flight
to continue their journey in life…
The squirrel in burrowing food for later use…
The tender new seedling reaching for the sunlight
to be nurtured as plants
producing their lovely flowers that we enjoy so much.

Such vitality and growth
to be accomplished during a short span of time.
Gaining strength to endure the upcoming hardships.

A plant, well fertilized,
is able to sustain itself during the dark and cold months.
Just as animal life, they too,
learn from their family how to survive the harsh times.

Nature's seasons over so fast.

To have the new born of spring getting ready for fall and winter so quickly.

Foliage and animal, both to prepare for survival in such a short time.

One to hide in the ground and others to flee south.

Both to find warmth and comfort during harsh times.

Isn't this as we do, just as the snowbirds?

# THE GOLDEN 50

Named after a most precious mineral,
in celebration of a long lifetime together.
To reflect upon the past,
look through the mirror of life and you will see
fond memories, sad moments, difficult times, love and hate,
all combined together.

What outshines all is your love for each other,
which must have been,
or it certainly would not have for 50 years.

The giving and unselfish persons willing to forgive one another,
moving on to enjoy and create the good times you have had.

Only such giving and special parents
will always have the devotion of their children.
Who, having the seeds of their thoughts and actions,
will always give back to them the same as they have been shown.

Thank you, for being mother and father, grandmother and
grandfather.

You are loved very much.

# KINDNESS

Kindness...Comes from the heart.
You do as much for yourself
as for those who receive it.

# UNCONDITIONAL LOVE

Your silent friend, life being a world far different from yours.
Always forever patient,
with never a complaint only showing affection towards you.

Happy with your touch and of just being close.
No words ever spoken.
A mutual feeling between the two of you.

Who is this perfect companion and friend for life?
For those who have one, it is very simple.
This could only be your pet.

# REFLECTIONS

To look into the mirror…do you like what you see?

Most will find flaws that we think all will see.
As we are judged upon by this.
Visual image, face, skin, body and dress.
What we are suppose to be.

Now, close your eyes. Look to your soul.
No one can see, but you.
No judgment, except from yourself.

Now, do you like what you see?
Reflections from yourself and no one else.

# INTERNET CONNECTION

An affair of the heart with someone unknown,
except through the sound of their voice
or the silent thought you have only read on your screen.

An easy way to express our feelings, to be heard and not seen.
No physical involvement or showing the signs of emotion
with perhaps flushing upon hearing a sexual statement.
Nor the possible trembling and quickened heart beat
upon a personal touch.

Yet, over time,
you build a longing or lust to be in contact with this person.
A natural instinct, the need for touch when there is desire.

Can technology fill this void
as we choose to hide behind the safety of the barriers available to us?
With only an exchange of thoughts.

Fantasy and then the need for reality.

# CALM

To sit and listen, but yet, all is so quiet.
Neither a sound nor breath of wind.
Calm in the air.
Not able to hear or feel what is around you.
Yet, such a tranquil feeling.

A much sought after moment.
Free from the everyday turbulence we encounter.
Our minds always busy with so many thoughts.
Dreams, expectations and goals to meet.

So yes, to be subdued with the tranquility and calm.
To capture the moment before the ever continuous storm.

# AS ONE

To be as mighty as the oak tree
reaching up to the sky. Spreading its strong limbs
to protect all below from an adverse environment.
Looking so powerful, such a majestic and natural strength.

Or, to be as the gentle willow tree.
Looking as if it feels such sorrow,
to lay down its limbs and gently weep.
To close into itself and surround others in its path for protection.
A much more humble of nature.

Both to be admired for their worthiness
that helps mold the world of what it is today.
Just as we are, all of a different being
surviving together.

The rainstorm together with the calm warmth
makes for the beauty of the rainbow we so much enjoy looking at.
Two different forces joined together end up with such a peaceful ending,

Joined together.

# THE SNOW BIRDS

Far away in distance, but still close to the heart.
Who are these people who have reached the age of retirement?

After working a lifetime, and serving their family or others, they
all seem to migrate to a warm climate.
Waking up to the warmth of the air and the
"What to do today attitude"

A tranquil time deserved.
They can forget the troubles in life they have encountered
and overcome.
To now enjoy what they have missed.

Perhaps to go to the beach, look out over the sea.
Finally, to hear the steady heartbeat, yet calm of the waves
as they wash ashore.
Nothing as tranquil as the finish
from the long journey they have endured.

Just as retirement, spending so many years to reach the shoreline.
When a time for tranquility and calm has been reached.

# NOW

Make the most of today as,
it will soon be yesterday
Only memories.

# THE HOUR GLASS

When young, the years pass by so slowly and we wish
tomorrow would come today in anticipation and excitement
of better things ahead.

Then, as we grow older, time goes by swiftly and hardly noticed.
Only to wish yesterday were today.
Realizing time is running out for what you might have changed.

The hourglass is not always predictable.
So we should not count the granules of sand left.
But, enjoy today for what it is.

Something we can change each day.
Tomorrow's yesterday is today's accomplishments and happiness.

# SUMMER'S END

How nice to sit and listen to the chirping of the birds,
as twilight nears.
Much for them to talk about before darkness falls.

To listen to the laughter and screams of the children in the distance.
All sounding alike…happiness in their voices.

Yes, for all to relish the short time left before fall and winter approach.
Bringing the cold winds and darkness.
A time when all seek shelter, whether it be inside your home or,
as nature does, burrowing into a safe, warm place.

A time for togetherness.

# THE ROSE

We all have expectations of what people & life should be.
Our own visualization.


Why is this?
Do we not want to see the truth at times?
It may be of an ugly picture.
So, we choose to paint over it, how we would like to see it.
A wishful fantasy.


The lovely scented flower is much better than a thistle with thorns.
Maybe we should bare ourselves to the thistle to see how the
thorns might hurt.
A few scratches and we may be stronger than we think.


Just as when you pick the lovely scented rose, you may also get
pricked by the thorn. A chance you must take.

# ALONE

A lonely old man, walking down the beach, thinks back on his life.
He was of strong character and expected as much from others.
He was not in need of any other.

And was unable to give kindness or feel compassion for any.
For they should all learn to be as he.

Maybe, he was a bit selfish and should have shown some compassion,
As his strength made others to feel inferior and weak

This man, will not receive from others that which he has not given.
For this, the lonely old man will now always walk alone.

Only his own set of footprints in the sand.

# JUDGMENT

What is it that makes us judge others so harshly
when we ourselves are not perfect?

Do we think that by stepping upon and hurting others,
we will make ourselves more powerful and mighty?

The old saying "Stones can break your bones but words never hurt"
I doubt to be true.

Words can hurt much more than the breaking of a bone.
A bone will heal swiftly
while the delicate mind may be wounded by rejection
having trouble finding the confidence to be of a worthy self.

Maybe, we should judge ourselves more carefully before we
step so harshly upon others.

# THE BLIND MAN

The man on the street always caries a bottle with his best friend in it.
Others carry theirs in different forms.
This friend helps him with laughter, jokes
and overcoming any failures or difficulties he may have.
His friend is always there when he needs him, never let down.

When he first met this friend, it was just for fun.
Now, he doesn't feel he could live without him.
Too many difficulties in life
Why put up with this yourself
when you have a friend that can make life look so much better?

So, he lives many years with this friend that he keeps a secret.
Other people don't have such friends that make them so happy.
Why share this with them?
They wouldn't understand.
It seems they have chosen a more difficult path
without the help of a best friend.

As the man grows into an old man, it seems he has become a bit blind.
His best friend now has to lead him along and live life for him.
This is much easier.
Maybe this friend has led him to this path of darkness.

# QUIET

Grasp the calm when you can.
Enjoy the silence,
hear the whistling of the wind or,
listen to the birds singing.

All so tranquil

# A CHILD'S ANGUISH

What's on My Mind?

Little things eat away at me.

No more am I able to just ignore my pain.

Each new thing adds to what is already the mountain.

Those that try to empathize, they have no idea.

I do not need fuel for my fire,

To be made angry over what I already despise.

I want a solution but there is none.

Why I am forgotten…what makes me so transparent?

Do I not work hard?

Do I not endeavor to reach my goals?

Is my goal not perfection?

But in my transparent state

maybe it is that they just don't see or they don't care.

So I continue as always…a ghost.

A memory of who is always forgotten.

My role is to continue on as I have.

Some day forgotten forever.

Why don't they just let me walk away?

# DEAR INVISIBLE,

If not recognized by someone we care about,
a person is left with an abandoned and unloved feeling.
With this, we tend to try to please others
in retaining our own confidence and self worth.

Your expectations may be set to high for the person
that is blinded by his own selfishness.
You are not invisible; this person cannot see you.
Someday, he may open his eyes in need of you or of your help.
It will be at this time that you may forgive him
and help to lead him from this path of darkness
or you can just let him walk away.

A memory to be forgotten…

# LIFE'S JOURNEYS

Do we not all go through hardships in life?
Maybe some of us have this of a gentle kind, others of a harsher.
No difference, to some what may be harsh is easy to another.

As if to pour salt on your wounds.
Does it hurt or do you know this is nature's way of healing.
The hurt at times may be your path to learning
the real wisdom that we all strive for.
Living through the pains and difficult times
pave our way to understanding.
Patience and knowledge that will make our lives easier.
It is this wisdom that only time and age can accomplish.

Just as our parents look at us.
A twinkle in their eye and warmth in their hearts.
To let us live and learn as they did.

# COURAGE

What courage it takes to challenge a new life, unknown.


The past, being of a sheltered and humble way.
Shelter in hiding and humble to ward off confrontations.
Knowing when to lay dormant during the difficult times.
Maybe to stay this way thus enabling others to thrive on your
weakness.
Their struggle for power.


If only life could be as simple as the sunrise.
To be seen on a clear day in all its beauty but to know it is still there,
to count on,
even when not seen on the overcast day.


Something forever, always able to depend on.

# ACCEPTANCE

Do we have to accept and find the good with everyone in life?
Or, is it better to lash out at the unacceptable?
By lashing out, we find an anger within us which can cause bitterness,
hard to get rid of.
It can grow, passing judgment upon others to harshly.

Maybe we can be a bit more compassionate
and overlook the flaws of others.

We are each our own person with a background and reason.
Who are we to judge the behavior of another being as acceptable or not?

Contentment will come when you are at peace with yourself.
Then you can accept others as they are.

You will not have to judge them, as they will judge themselves.

# REMINISCE

To sit and meditate thinking back on your past.
Joy, sorrow, regret, happiness.
Just living without much thought.

As the years pass, time seems to sneak by us so quickly.
With regret now in taking for granted
our daily journeys that are running out.

Slow down and enjoy what is here today.

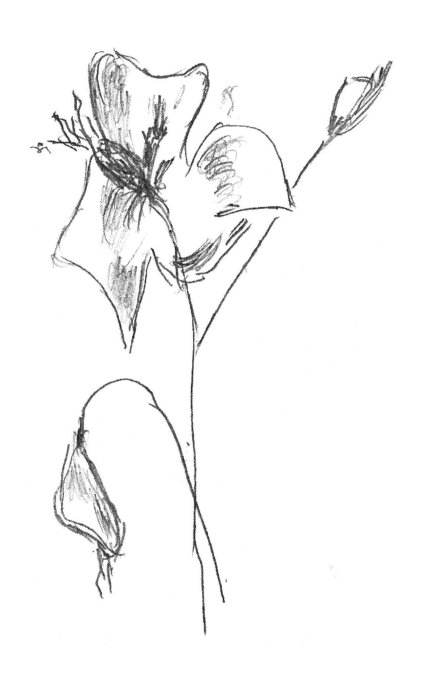

# THE WISE OLD WOMAN

The old woman sits down to rest
with nothing but her clothing on her back
and a flower in her hand.
She looks around and sees.

She sees the busy people, hears the noise of the traffic
and smells the pollution.
She lifts the flower to her nose and smiles.
No, she is not going to close her eyes on life
to dwell on the many injustices
and low times she has been through.
She has lived a long life and will think back
to the many happy times.

She sees a young man who seems very sad.
Does he think only his life is troublesome?
She walks over to this young man and hands him her flower.
He looks up and smiles.

Now, maybe, she has helped him to see.

# FORGET ME NOT

| | |
|---|---|
| Botanical Name: | Anchusa Capensis |
| Common Name: | FORGET ME NOT |
| Outstanding Characteristics: | Hardy plant. |
| | Can thrive in any condition. |
| | Needs little care. |

Young children so dependent upon you.
The years of nurturing, forming a bond.
Over time, this bond is broken
as the child turns into an adult.
To have their own life.
Trying to live up to expectations.
In the process, turning away from dependency,
breaking the bond.
This is part of growing up; however…
Your family if like the plant.
Not requiring much but if uncared for
will wither away.

FORGET ME NOT.

# CHOICES

When young, life seems so perfect.
Has it really been?
Have you found ways in which to hide imperfections?
Do you choose to overlook that which is burdensome or
try to change it?

To overlook may not be so bad.
Life is too short to some and not worth the effort.
To others, to change that which they feel is wrong is a battle to be won.

I guess each person must follow his path.
Along this path, the man without shoes will toughen his soles in battle,
Or if he chooses, will soften them in overlooking while treading softly.

Neither right nor wrong, just a choice.

# THE BLADE OF GRASS

Life is like a blade of grass.
The storms will come and they will pass.
In the beginning you plant a seed.
You water and water and sometimes feed.
In the end it will grow old then die,
or maybe the sun will slowly fry.
It's too bad it has to be that way.
I wish I could live life day to day.

# THE SEED

You talk of a seed of grass which we all come from.
Yes, the storms do come and we lie flat against the wind.
When the storm is over, we spring to life again.
This is the way of life!
We protect ourselves against the powers we cannot control
and when in control, we spring back.
Don't you know?
A blade of grass is stepped upon, moved and overtaken by weeds.
But do you see the grass die?
No, you see the grass overcome the elements of nature
and it always springs back to life.
In fact, it doesn't even grow old, it grows more course,
harder to destroy.

Experiences in life are often difficult, other times joyful.
We fall with storms and spring back with the calm

So, I guess we do live day by day.
You don't have to wish it, because it has been true.

# DEAR FRIEND

So many years to pass, without seeing or talking to one another.
However, having many happy thoughts of you from the past.

How many times was I to pick up the phone to call, but didn't.
To find out later this was during your darkest time in life.
A time of need and I of no help and not knowing.

However, as you know,
you have never really been without a true and faithful friend.
One who is always there, the friend who carried you,
leaving only his set of footprints.

Yes, I am sorry I was not there also.
Yet if ever another time in need,
I would like to be the second set of footprints
to walk along with you and your friend.

# THE YOUNG BOY

Once, a little boy with blond hair and blue eyes.
So innocent, full of questions in experiencing life
and only a few answers given by the parents, when time.

So, the little boy sets out
to find his own answers and a direction in life.
Along this path, he will encounter many obstacles.
Some of which will enhance his later life and
some of which will change his life.

It is during this time that we form our own self
and at an early age this self is still innocent enough to change.
We don't want the path to be so difficult so that we stop exploring.
The tiring of uphill or downhill
but rather the flat even ground, as an easier route.

Maybe, a parent should share their experiences
in the difficult paths they have traveled,
helping the child in choosing the right one.

The little boy with blond hair and blue eyes grows older.
With help in his direction, the young man is now
walking the flat even ground.

# HAPPY ANNIVERSARY

Are we still in harmony?
I think so.

You lead this time and I'll follow.
We'll keep the dance going
until the music fades.

We'll have the last dance together.

# ABOUT THE AUTHOR

Judy was born in Seattle, Washington and still lives nearby. She has one child, now grown, and a husband. Judy keeps busy with a business she started many years ago and in her spare time, doodles around writing poems. Thus, the nickname assigned to her by her family is "Doodles."

What has inspired Judy is her love for nature, the innocence and purity of it. Having spent summers at their seaside cabin was such a treat. Those are her most cherished memories and although that time is past, putting those memories to paper rekindles those peaceful moments and brings a smile to her inner self. Judy hopes that her poems are enjoyed by her readers as much as she has enjoyed writing them.

# THOUGHTS AND SECOND THOUGHTS

## By Barry Clapsaddle

From the claustrophobic dreams and interminable drudgery of a worker in the not too distant future to a young man's fantasies about a sexy convicted killer, the stories in *Thoughts and Second Thoughts* portray people caught up with both themselves and their situations, sometimes of their own making and sometimes not, but caught nonetheless. Influenced by an eclectic literary heritage, Barry Clapsaddle describes, among other stories, the indelible antics of some oddball street cops and the vagaries of modern warfare with equal insight and intensity. Combining experiences and creativity, the vignettes in this collection offer glimpses into and raise questions about life and death and the struggles in between, in settings that gradually fade into their own, often roughhewn backgrounds, but told always with the quick wink and nod of a crafted storyteller.

*Paperback, 57 pages*
*6" x 9"*
*ISBN 1-4137-8601-4*

**About the author:**

In addition to *Thoughts and Second Thoughts*, Barry Clapsaddle has written two screenplays, *Elysian Fields* and *Picking Up the Pieces*. He has undergraduate and graduate degrees in literature, and is the President and CEO of the IT firm CTGi. He lives near Washington, D.C., with his wife, Laura, and their four children.

Also available from PublishAmerica

# DAY OF THE SHADOW
## By Ronald W. Knott

Meet Joseph Parrot, a Native American living in
the Canadian northwest. An ordinary man with a
bit of history, he thought his dreams were dead at
age forty-two, with a family and working as a
simple surveyor of the land. A highschool
sweetheart, now an FBI agent, comes knocking,
offering Joe the job of a lifetime…tracking
terrorists that have eluded the Feds with their
intentions for years. Joe was unknowingly
groomed for two years by the FBI. Now with
wife Hanna's blessing, a bad relationship with
teenage daughter Cameron and mother Twila
suffering from Alzheimer's, he is off to track the
enemy around the world. Traveling from Hong
Kong to London and on to Moscow, he ultimately
interrupts the successful takeover of the entire
nuclear arsenal! Joe Parrot returns home a
wounded and changed man to a surprise ending.

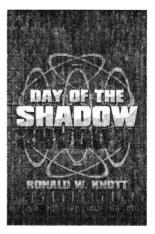

*Paperback, 295 pages*
*6" x 9"*
*ISBN 978-1-60749-188-0*

**About the author:**

I published my memoir, *Jaundiced*, with PublishAmerica, and wrote three
feature screenplays including *Day of the Shadow*. I had a part in the movie
*The Alphabet Killer* starring Timothy Hutton and Eliza Dushku. I am Native
American and currently work as a behavioral health technician. I live with
my wife, Carol-Aynn, in Rochester, New York.

Available to all bookstores nationwide.
www.publishamerica.com